Bycatch

Bycatch

Caroline Smith

Nine
Arches
Press

Bycatch
Caroline Smith

ISBN: 978-1-916760-28-8
eISBN: 978-1-916760-29-5

First published October 2025 by:

Nine Arches Press
Studio 221, Zellig
Gibb Street, Deritend
Birmingham
B9 4AU
United Kingdom
www.ninearchespress.com

Printed in the United Kingdom on recycled paper by:
Imprint Digital

Nine Arches Press is supported using public funding by Arts Council England.

Supported using public funding by
**ARTS COUNCIL
ENGLAND**

To my sister Hilary and brother Justin:
for all the hours we shared caring for our parents.

Contents

IV. Protest

V. Hope

VI. Grace

Dedication

I lost a pound note
I'd been given as a child
and you gave me half back,
to teach me to be careful
but to mitigate my loss.
When you were old
but could still drive,
and I locked myself out,
you came half the distance
to bring me your key.
As pieces of you are lost
one by one, and the parts
of this book build into a whole.
I give you back
an approximation of your life
to meet you half way.

I.

Removal

Noah

I chart my parents' decline
by how far the answer machine gets
before one of them reaches the phone.
Tonight,
the whole recording plays through
and they do not answer.

I imagine it ringing
in the dusk of their living room,
newspaper spread out,
pages divided up between them.
His head is back in the chair,
mouth ajar, feet turned out on the stool.

She will be dozing
on her side on the sofa
knees up, hands folded under her face,
crossword half-finished next to her.
They'll fumble under the paper for the handset,
befuddled at having slept into evening.

The distances they could walk
just a few months ago,
are now an ocean for them to cross.
And I am Noah, waiting for their call back.
I've sent out a dove to find land.
One day it won't return.

Path

The house is testing them.
Their strategies for survival
becoming visible: pliers left out –
to peel back yoghurt pot lids.

We found my father
climbing the steep stairs,
dog lead clipped, one end to his belt,
the other to the handrail.
Cushions arranged over food-stained seats.

And now as I swivel round
the heavy ring on their back door,
I stoop into the deep cold
of an unlocked church.

I shovel a thick fleece of ash
from the hearth and tramp out
in the icy blue of a still evening
in search of logs.

It's dark when I leave them
wrapped up before a fire.
As I make it down the path
resolving to phone the estate agent,

I look back across
the white hostile ground
to the strip of light under their door –
and the two pairs of shoes
placed neatly outside.

Removal

Landlords are shifting out old tenants.
It's the season of mattresses.
Checked, stained,
they are dumped in the road overnight.
Cramped in half,
their split seams erupt yellow foam
like crops of toadstools
under this grey wash
of a Middlesex autumn sky.

A piece of dark cloth is tacked to the window
of the maisonette my pregnant friend
is viewing to buy – her first home.
The tenant has been issued a Section 21
and won't answer the door,
so we can only get access
now the owner's swept in to open up.
The tenant follows us from room to room
leaning her cheek against the door frame,
watching. It's the same stare
I saw on my father's ivory face.

I was digging up plants from his garden,
he'd agreed I could,
after finally accepting
he had to move.
I thought he was asleep,
but he'd followed me out
shuffling slowly after me.
He stood balancing with his two sticks,
just watching at a distance
from the middle of the path.

Blazer

Foremost in his wardrobe now, the black tie –
already worn three times this month.

He rises in the early morning.
It takes him an hour these days to get ready.

Stiffeners flick from his collar and spin across the room.
He bends slowly to pick them up.

Today he is dressing for his old colleague,
in the ancient blazer with the brass anchor buttons,

the one he bought himself with his first pay rise.
It flaps loosely, slipping off one shoulder.

He's searching the pockets for the letter
his friend had forged from 'Simpsons of Piccadilly'

requesting he return the blazer to the store
for a larger size, 'to preserve their reputation'.

Thinks he'll use the joke in his tribute.
He's kept it forty-seven years –

the envelope with the letter he'd found
propped on his desk when he got back from lunch.

Everyone in the office, heads down
hard at work.

Muster

I arrive unexpectedly
find them mustered in the kitchen.
The dishwasher on its drying cycle
patters like heavy rain.
My father is using his stick and the wall
to keep steady, hooking open the door,
bailing things out
through the hot gush of steam.
He passes the milk jug to my mother,
she takes it and rests it on the bin,
then edges to the cupboard.
The crew are struggling.
I clear the debris from the squall
and take them, exhausted, back to shore.

Last Stand

We've been here since dawn,
cleaning to make the house presentable
for the buyers, who are back for one last look.
We had Dad holed up in the kitchen,
but he's broken out and against all instruction,
is telling the surveyor, 'It does have its problems'.
He was the same at their interview
for the retirement village
when he kept asking over and over,
'Is there an emergency doctor on site?'
He scuppered the last sale,
talking about the dormouse they'd found
paddling in the toilet, and how, even though
they'd fished it out with a colander,
and laid it on the grass, it had died anyway.
The surveyor says, he'll show himself round, 'thank you'.
But Dad is hobbling slowly down
through the long overgrown garden,
to point out where the septic tank
seeps up into the grass.

Lemon Tea

I'm not sure when the Teasmaid
stopped being a part of their lives.
A procession of brown stained china sets
had sat by their bed for over thirty years.
But before the Teasmaid, on Saturdays,
I would help Dad make Mum breakfast in bed.
I'd stand on the stool by the sink,
while he made toast high up under the grill.

One side would always burn,
and he'd lob it to me,
black one side, spongey white the other.
I would scrape and scratch with my knife
and blow black powder to settle on the water.
Once when we ran out of milk
he made her tea with a lemon
and gave me half to suck coated in sugar.

Today he stands all oddly,
one arm dangling by his side,
still making her tea.
I watch him lift out the tea bag
by its corner, drawing it up
like a squid rising through sea.
And then he lobs it into the sink
and it's that action I remember –

him lobbing slices of half-burnt toast,
and the lemon
that left a wince and ache in my mouth.

Shed

Not treasure, just old things
here in the repository
of all they've discarded over the years.
A freezer that doesn't shut,
the shopping trolley they used
for ferrying food from car to house.
A stack of LPs
balances on a rusted BBQ.
I separate the top one,
stuck with spoors and dust.
The heavy buckled vinyl
is fused to the yellowed sleeve.
On the cover,
a picture of the White House.
It's an RCA Victor recording:

'Inspirational Expressions after the death
of President John F Kennedy'.

I'm playing quietly
under the table
stacking my father's shiny
white horseshoe collars.
I'm watching him
staring into the television set
with its thin tripod legs:
the deep sea-green bowl,
its two Bakelite dials,
the glitter canvas webbing.
I'm scared by his sadness,
by the gloom descended on the house
and the fish eaten in silence for days.

The Ring

My final job in the still house is to look for
my mother's eternity ring. I pull back
grey lips of carpet, poke behind radiators,
draw up stockings of cobwebs and ease out
the bright eye of a ballpoint pen.
Eventually I lock up and make a last trip
to the skip, through the apples
lying in the long grass, the bean canes
spiralling with bindweed.
All the tension of a quest is gone –
a slack journey back through abandoned lands
of pink-tailed mint and patches of nettles.

II.

Taking Leave

Seeds

My father is bereft of his garden.
And as I cross the grounds
of the retirement village
I see his stooped figure under his hat.
He's struggling to plant seeds
in the shingly borders of the communal paths.

I picture our visits to Great Aunt Madelaine
and the Giant Hogweed – seeds
lodged in the pocket of a brother
returning from war.
They'd spread from her homestead
out across the fields and lanes.

We would dodge the blistering sap
of the towering umbels
as we played in the ramshackle garden
and she watched from the door,
shielding her face
from an accidental sighting of the moon.

As I greet my father, trowel in hand,
he slowly straightens up.
One day soon
these paths will be bright with his Clarkia
and I'll recall how we once looked out
for the furthest outriders of the Hogweed.
And navigate my way on.

Links

On damp days like this
he doesn't want to go out.
All he wants to do is sleep.
But I make him come for a walk
and help him on with his coat,
lifting the heavy bottle-green jacket
over his back.
He grips the lining of one sleeve
and threads back through, the other arm.
Outside the aftermath of rain, bright
and fresh, drips into the water butt
and pools on the path.
His arm is looped through mine.
The brush of our coats as we walk
is the rustle of loose paper chains.
I remember him telling me once,
as I stood on a chair,
draping paper tresses
from the corners of the ceiling,
how he'd loved being on the farm,
but his parents had brought them
back to London despite the bombs,
because they'd lost the child allowance
while they were away.
And how it was hot summer
but the Christmas decorations were still up.

Last Vaudeville

Eventually we get Dad down into the boat
where he loudly invites all the elderly ladies
to a seat on his lap
'as the benches are so squashed'.
He is talking too much –
it's the joy of a captive audience
but he's been off the boards too long
and needs to rediscover his art.

The boat swivels off in a flourish,
a dark caliper of water widening from his stage
and him spotlit in a column of sun.
He jokes that I will steal the
water spaniel's muzzle to put on him,
but his words come out jumbled
and all the owner hears is
'She's going to steal your dog'.

I look for something to distract him
but the landscape is still and serene.
Just waders stalking the estuary shoreline
prodding and stuttering the mud.
Geese are hawking from distant fields
as a whine of swans' wings
grinds overhead like some creaking stage
machinery wound with old handles.

And it's all become part of Dad's
impromptu vaudeville act.
He's animated. And as we finally dock,
I'm reluctant to pull him away.
But like an old sly dog, yanking his lead
to snatch at a crimson chicken bone,
he twists out of his collar
and turns back for an encore.

Taking Leave

His brother is sitting by the window.
The nurse has tipped a jigsaw puzzle
on the table in front of him,
clumps of grey cardboard, a twiggy heap
nobbled as the oak leaves
thick under the trees in the grounds outside.
My father struggles slowly through the Day Room
lifting his stick as he looks around smiling.
His brother has been told he is coming
but beams in surprise when he sees him.

I get some chairs. I want it to be special,
an exchange of stories from
the deep sequestration of ninety years
but they say almost nothing
just find each other's shaking hand.
We sit in the winter Sunday afternoon
and although we could stay longer, until the bell,
and even knowing this is the last time,
they are tired,
and they've said all there is to say.

Listening

Each time I speak to the Home Office
about the KIU/arrivals stuck in the local Budget Plaza,
an advert for the hotel pops up on my phone.

It's the one I booked my parents into
for the wedding, before my father had a stroke.
I'd taken them as close as I could,

they'd struggled from the car over the paved mall
wheeling their huge suitcases. Returning, I found them
waiting by the self-check-in of the deserted foyer.

They couldn't get the knack
of catching down the key card to unclasp
the heavy fire doors or open the lift.

They moved so slowly along the eighth-floor corridor
every bend turning into another long passage of doors
each lit above with a dim lantern.

The small room with the sealed window had no phone
and as I settled them, my mother had asked

'Will anyone know we're here?'

KIU = Kent Intake Unit

Coda

Every few months
my father remembers his violin.
We will take down the case
and snap the locks sideways,
blow dust off
the cracked red varnish.
I lift it, so light,
from the frayed green silk
and hold it on my knee,
supporting its neck
as I pluck and tune loose strings
and place it under his chin.

The bow finds the old groove
in the rosin, deep as a cart rut,
releasing the scent of a pine forest
cooling after a hot day.
I try to steady his hand
resting the bow on the strings.
He's listening acutely
for the sounds of birdsong
returning in the evening shade,
a siskin dipping between the trees,
hovering
like his once good bowing arm.

Chrism

Her back has shrunk away from her bra
like dried-out soil from the sides of a pot.
The ancient cups hang free from her shoulders.
The wonky row of bra extenders
she's added over time
to help her reach to the clasp behind, are like
the overlapping Green Shield stamps
stuck together in rows
in the buckled, tea-stained Co-op book
that we filled up and took in to exchange
for the luxury we couldn't afford.
With one hand, my father is rubbing precious oil
into my mother's stiff, stooped shoulder.
The other balances unsteadily on his stick.

Shoes

Mine got wet whilst out walking
so my mother went to find me a pair of hers.
But she's put them down somewhere
and now can't find them.
Dad picks up that we are looking for shoes
and sees mine drying.
'There are shoes there, are they the ones?'
'No', I say 'they are my wet ones'.
'Which ones have you lost?' he asks.
'My black ones', Mum says loudly
stressing the syllables.
'Black ones?'
And he starts round the flat,
slowly searching for shoes.
'There are some there.'
He is looking at a giant pair
of dark brown ones, with wide tan welts.
'But those are yours, Dad.'
I see him moving shoes around with his stick.
He hangs onto this idea of shoe
as if it were a tugboat
guiding him through fog.

Twin Tub

Anxious, just home from school,
I would push open the back door
into the fug and noise of the twin tub
pulled out into the middle of the kitchen.
Under the lid of the washer,
blistered soapy clothes would be slowly stewing.
I liked to prod them back under
with the bleached silver driftwood tongs
then watch my mother haul them over
in a thick sopping plait
to slither into the spinner.

The spinning tub would jump and judder
and rattle itself across the floor.
When it came to a stop,
she peeled out clothes plastered round the inside.
Mum was always stern on wash days,
as she is now, watching my father
stooped over the washing machine
struggling to open the door and push in
his wetted trousers with the butt of his stick.
She refuses to do it for him,
because he refuses to wear pads.

Breath

I cover the cold V of his neck
and leave my father to sleep.
His stick rests against the chair,
hands loose-fisted but fitful.
Outside, cars light up the road,
a red pool behind, gold in front.
I tiptoe away, that long walk
I've done over the years
across my children's bedroom,
chest tightening
on every creaking board.
At the door I turn
the way I always did,
door latch suspended,
unable to leave
until I'd gone back
one last time to check.

III.

Archaeology

Late

I hesitate to push too hard
on this unsteady gate,
try to lift it carefully
into the stories
from my father's early life.
Fretting against his lapsing memory,
cursing myself as I did as a child
always leaving my chores too late
until the grass was long
and the job much harder.
And I'd have to drag the big mower
back and forwards, whirring against
hidden edges of paving slabs.
But it was summer
the sun warm
the spokes of lavender full
and I was busy building tracks
through the rockery for matchbox cars,
running them behind falls of aubretia
under the sleepy eye of the toad
that sat beneath a craggy overhang
snapping at fruit flies
in the purple flowering thyme.

Bike

Somewhere it still lies,
wheel buckled, pedal jutting up
among purple quilted nettles
latched over by ivy
its heavy black paintwork
slowly corroding.
And as I pull upon the story,
I uncover the yellowed imprint
cut deep into my grandfather's life.
A young lad with a shiny new bike,
his brother Philip, had begged him
for a ride, just once,
before he went off to war.
My grandfather had refused
and when the telegram came
stamped his foot through the spokes.

Archaeology

'When I first went to Germany after the war,
I was quite shy. Got bullied a lot ....'

His opening halts me.
Like an old wall in the middle of a field,
there's no path beyond it, nothing it connects to.

I'm asking my father about his National Service.
But I know this story, the one he'll slip into telling:

how he once stood up to the popular bully
on the RAF base, challenged him to a fight
and how, when they finally called a truce,
'shook hands and became the best of friends'.

It's a great story,
but there's always been something about it
of the *Boy's Own* tales he loved.
The unlikely hero, who'd pull through,
and right would always win.

I feel like an interrogator trying to establish who,
seventy years ago, he really was.
And I'm reluctant to pull too hard.
These artefacts are held together
by both bindweed and honeysuckle.

Some days it seems there is just an outline left
of what shaped his life –
a few bricks covered in green moss.
They could be significant – or just a wall.

Evacuees

Everything is told as it has always been:
the half-moon marks
made by the agitated horses
backing across the cobbled yard.
The blacksmith, still irritably
wading over in his split leather apron
with flaming tongs;
halters twisted round the fence post
in the trodden corner of the field
and the scattered rinds of hoof clippings.

Was it this year or that year
when he shook out pale slabs of hay
into the troughs,
the sweet dry smell of evening
the horses pulling out wisps with blunt teeth?
When he slept on top of a pile of mattresses
and slept so deeply
in the countryside blackout,
in the farmhouse box room,
away from the noise and terror of London?

Nothing more or less
is ever told of this story
just the same few fragments
left for me to colour in.
The last evacuees to be picked
because there were two of them;
how the brothers perched on the back
of the jolting cart and rattled
through the darkening fields
from Tiverton station to the farm.

Woolwich Ferry

The three of us would be laid out
in the back of the old Singer Gazelle
with pillows and blankets, the seat down flat
for the journey back from our grandparents.
And as we passed the site of the Express Dairy
we'd ask Dad for *the story* again.

His voice strangely low,
carried along with the grind of gears,
the streetlights' tired glow above;
I would imagine the milkman
trying to harness the heavy dray,
oddly skittish in the eerie dawn.

'Something that day spooked the big horse,
caused it to bolt down Ilford High Road'.

I pictured the great beast scraping the ground
with its huge, tented hoof,
lip curled back, grey neck foaming,
the milk cart careening from side to side.

'And then a policeman, your grandfather,
leapt into the path of the runaway and caught up the reins'.

Perhaps it was at that point in the journey,
that we reached the ferry, and the rattle of ramps,
the weathered shouts and strained grey faces
of the night dockers –

but Dad could never bring himself to finish the story.
The part where my grandmother, who saw it all,
fell in love with the brave young officer.
And how she'd come back every day
to cross the road on his beat, and how
he'd stop the traffic with his white baton, just for her.

Hephaestus the Smith

My grandmother dreams
>> of the strong young police officer.

She dreams of flaming hooves
>> of beating temples and golden chariots.

She will catch and marry him.
>> He will take her away
>>> from the orphanage.

She leaps
>> into the turquoise and gold
>>> and they begin the steep climb
>>>> of married life.

But the gap starts to widen between
>> sky and ground
>> the beasts of
>>> war and poverty rise.

They cannot steer Apollo's bolting steeds
>> or find the narrow path
>>> to happiness.

My father, a young child
>> will task himself with
>>> gathering up the wreckage
>>>> of the fallen sun chariot.

He will bend out buckled, tangled iron,
>> strewn through their lives,
>>> will weld it into something new.

Ellen Maud Smith

Once her telephone was installed, my father's
aunt would phone him all through the night

There was no music at her brief committal.
Seven in attendance, two nurses and us
in the small church in the Essex village
where Ellen was born and lived all her life.
The only daughter amid six sons,
she'd cared for her parents and her last brother,
and then, when none of the village boys
came back from the war, lived on
in the dwelling sunk behind a now busy road,
among cow parsley and tottering beehives.
She'd often tell of the day
she won first prize at the singing gala
in the summer church fete.
How she'd sung Ave Maria in her bonnet and ribbons
her voice sweet as a green linnet
above the upturned faces of that afternoon.
How she'd skipped home in the cooling sun
black-blue swallows skimming
evening insects off the long pale grass –
the lights coming on in the village
and her whole life ahead.

Southend-on-Sea

In summer we went to the seaside
on a double-decker train.
I lay under the deckchairs
beneath the massive shapes
of my grandparents' oblong rumps,
a row of them
pressing through the canvas
blocking the sun.
I'd doodle my fingers
through silk pools of grey sand,
cool in the shady patches under the seats,
where I lay hidden
among the toe-stubbing struts
half buried, lopsided by their weight,
watching sun
dappling through the gaps.

We would linger until evening
when the dark would
come down in blocks, suddenly.
Time to drag cold towels
coated and heavy as wet breaded fish,
accelerating our pace
through sinking shadowy sand
sharp spikes of marram,
nails of shell
and black twists of bladderwort
crisp as lambs' umbilical cords,
the day's spell broken.
Anxious then, as I am now,
hurrying across a causeway
to get back to you,
while there's still time.

IV.

Protest

Visiting

My father has become an old Aegean King
peering out anxiously,
scanning the horizon full of foreboding.
So I phone him before I leave
to say I'm on my way.
I use light words, 'coming soon',
'around that time', promising words
that hover and play, allow him
to drift in and out of sleep
while he waits,
the way he did on the lake front
that year, filling whole mornings
just sitting, watching
for the small island ferry.
He'd listen to the early wash of pebbles,
the bakery opening,
the few passengers beginning to assemble.
The lake was so still, so flat,
he could follow the ferry's whole journey –
see it set off from the far shore,
its flourishes in and out of tiny bays.
And wake to its arrival.

Beds

It was less than a year ago
the estate agent lay down on the floor
in the odd shaped bedroom
to prove it would take a double bed.
We, indignant, reproachful –
our parents had slept in the same bed
together for sixty-six years.
But now we've moved Mum
into a single bed in the living room
because Dad shouts out all night
and social services have wheeled in
a hospital-bed with a hoist.
Dad's lifted in and out
in a builders' sack
like a cubic measurement of sand.

Disorientation

Today it's the sales patter
my father wants me to fall for –
the road contractor with excess shingle
to offload on a Friday night in a quick
cash-in-hand deal.
'Look. If you take me home now
before it gets dark, you can be back
in time for tea.'
He pushes hard with his offer.
'Just get the keys will you?'
Already tipping up his lorry in the driveway,
he unstraps his chair
his breath the coarse scrape of a spade
in the scrunch of orange shingle.

Another day he will reason,
'It can't be our home,
kitchen's in the wrong place.
Odd though
it does have the same furniture as ours.
It's even got our pictures.'
'Stay in your chair',
my mother shouts.
'I can't pick you up if you fall.'
He's stranded within the misaligned
layout of the retirement flat
on an ancient migration path,
the route home
blocked by new roads and fences.

Shower

He slipped over in the shower.
They found him wrapped
in the cold clinging curtain
the pole pulled down.
The paramedics say they'll have to
take him into hospital if he tries
to get out of bed again on his own.
It's the third time he's got up early
to wash himself
before the carers come in.

The Multiverse

'I've found you a car'
Dad says.
'I cut out the advert
from the back of the magazine
and put it on the piano.
I think you'll like this one.
Get it will you?'

I say, 'I'll look a bit later'.
But he's insistent and I agree to get it.
'It will suit you nicely,' he says.
I hope my father will forget
when I leave the room,
but I can hear him shouting
'Can you bring it through?'

I go back to him – he is
plucking at his covers,
pushing around the bolsters
trying to raise himself up.
'Sorry Dad, I couldn't find it.'
'But I put it on the piano
when we went to the cottage for a night.'

'It must have been tidied away,' I say
'because it's not there anymore –
But tell me about the car'.
'It was grey' he says.
'Was it like your car?'
But he begins to mumble and
the cars drive off in different directions.

Bibs

He won't wear the bibs
the carers asked us to get.
And I'm reminded of the story
he told us once,
about the old couple,
made to eat from a trough
by their children.
One day the old man
had gone slowly out to the shed,
found some pieces of wood
nails and a hammer.
The children asked what he was making.
He told them,
'A trough for you, for when you are old'.

Protest

'So they got you too, did they?'
he asks when I visit.
My father thinks he's in prison.
'Your mother's in the next cell down.
Aren't you?' he shouts.

He is agitated, gripping the bed bars
trying to get up.
Every day his pads are dry
but at night he rips them off,
soils the sheets and covers.

The carers have blamed chocolate ice cream
and forbidden it.
He is losing weight rapidly.
No time to coax him to eat
in their short-allotted visits, so he goes without.

After they have gone, my mother
lies next to him and holds his hand.
She slowly feeds him white Magnums
that she thinks won't be detected –
or traced back to her.

Peas

Completing a Care Commission application:
Evidence is required of when your condition first began.

We were sitting on the doorstep
shucking peas in the sun.
Just the snap of pods,
slit of our nails in the crushed green tops.
Peas rattling into the colander –
                              our crisscrossing hands.
Then
    I saw your growing confusion
between the piles.
And my thumb jerked a row,
buckling peas like a lorry cab jack-
                              knifing.

Printer

Suddenly, randomly
throughout the day
the printer starts up,
lurching into action
laboriously printing nothing
before settling restlessly.
The way my father,
with small bursts of effort
will clutch at the sides of his bed
trying to lift himself out,
before sinking back.

Gift

The Kesar mangoes are angled in a box
in their orange diamond stretched vests.
I hold one up in my palm,
peel puckered skin and shave off slivers
down to the wispy stone.
It is wet and tufted as a shaken dog
plastered hair clinging to thin bone.
I take through a bowl and fork
and tuck a towel around his neck.
He rises forward from his bed
like a carp in an ornamental pond
where they hang from the surface,
orange robed monks, hoop mouths open wide.
I lay a wafer of mango on his tongue.

Changing the Bed

From outside in the grounds
he hears the squeak of a wheelbarrow.
Nurses roll him on his side.

'One.... Two....' They whisk out the Kylie sheet.

He feels the heavy handles of the barrow,
steers it through the farmyard to the midden
running up the plank to tip up another load.

The scrape of his shovel
across the orange-soaked flagstones
pitching in soiled straw and olive dung –

and the tea put on for them
in the village hall, when they'd finished
and went back to their billets.

'That's better. We'll leave you for now then.'

He shakes out straw across the stall. The bed feels fresh,
where a horse in the yard kicks the door impatiently
and a swallow dips into the open barn.

Walking Stick

....
    'I've polished up your stick.'

'It was your dad's – remember?
        .... that first date with Mum?
when you were just back from National Service?
        .... and Grandad followed you to the Troxy?'

I pause to see if he remembers why he's kept the stick all his life.
Why, all dusty, grey and rubber-end cracked as a dog's dry nose,
it was his favourite.

        .... 'Your dad sat four rows behind and prodded you with it
all through the film. He offered you sweets and an orange?
        .... But Mum fell for you anyway.'

I leave time for the story to sink in,
        the way I'd left the wax to soak into the wood
– pale and naked when stripped of its dark varnish.
        I'd scoured it with wire wool,
working to bring back the memory in the grain.

Mealtimes

Today they came at 9:00 to make breakfast
then back at 10:30 to give him lunch.

Now the long stretch.

He knows these hours of waiting –
the randomness of meals.

All the fights between his parents
had coalesced around mealtimes.

That last evening before he ran away
he'd tipped up the dish of food
they were rowing over.

They'd both looked up in fury.
It was the only time he ever saw them united.

Transfiguration

He's looking at us
with wild eyes and tangled beard
and clutching the sides of the bed.
He winces as the razor clicks
against the basin like a thrush
cracking a snail on a slab.
Open fingers gently press down
and direct his head.

'I'm in agony' – he whispers.

'You're killing me.'

Then he makes the sound I heard
when my cat caught a bird –
the low yowl in the throat –
a haunting wail.

Plums

When he tells me one day

'I feel happy'

My heart shifts the heavy branch
broken off last year, overladen with fruit
that has slumped under cowls of moss
and wet leaves.

He has found for me
the tiny plums fused to the stalks,
fluorescent blue, midnight lapis
set in copper filigree.

Ocean World

It's the gloom
of an end of pier aquarium
surrounded by open sea.
I find him thrashing in bed
unable to turn
pulling away the grey cot bumpers
that protect his contracted leg.
I stroke his rough cold forehead
and get his box of tissues.

There's a hollow magnified rasp
as he pulls them continuously
and tears them into white shreds.
I open my hand and he carefully
places them in my palm.
We sit and exchange them
over and over
it's the echo of surf, the tiny laps
breaking and closing.

Flowers

I put a swerve of daffodils into a vase
and snip the blue band
low waisted like a flapper dress.
They splay open, firm triangular stems.
I squeeze in a pouch of salts
squirting hard against the sides,
like an udder clouding the water,
and take them through to his room.

The house is filling up with flowers
standing in buckets, the air warm,
fragrant, full of moisture,
a temperate zone.
He has tipped over a reef
into a tranquil morphine lagoon.

V.

Hope

The Memory Game

My mother phones and asks for:
a sack of bird seed,
a birthday card with a Collie on it
and some full cream milk.
I say, 'Don't you need any food?'
She says she is 89 years of age
and knows what she needs.
The next day she rings my brother
and says she must have some bread.
Then she calls my sister to tell her
'I have no food in the house'.
I'm in the queue with the shopping
when my phone rings.
'Where are you?'
'I'm shopping Mum.
Is everything ok?'
'Did you remember my torch?'

White Out

Thick snow has fallen through winter.
It has smoothed over the tracks and dips
and caverns of his speech.
His thoughts flattened to a white plane.
The glare bewilders.
All directions look the same.
All clues muffled.
My mother talks about normal.
'As soon as we're back to normal.'
She talks about their life together
imagines it is still there underneath
waiting for them again in the spring.

Care Assessment

An assessor makes an unannounced visit
and asks my mother
what my father can do.
My mother says yes to everything
and later phones
to tell me she thinks he's passed.

Handkerchiefs

The ironing board leans against
the bathroom wall, one strut jutting
like the trailing legs of a heron.

I ratchet it together and let it drop open.
Thin halva yellow foam slips out
from under the layers of scorched covers.

I get my father's white handkerchiefs
stiff and pointed as starfish
from where they've been pegged above the bath.

She lifts the iron slowly over the big misshapen squares.
It's her last resistance against the carers
who bring him boxes of tissues

and every day wash his drip-dry sheets,
which air like slack sails,
hanging over every door in the flat.

His handkerchiefs were the first thing
my mother taught me to iron; and now
the last of his things she can manage.

She stands at the ironing board
a captain in full uniform,
refusing to leave her ship.

Dying

My mother phones and says she thinks
my father's dying. She is crying,
says there's been a change.
I rush over. I'm crying
and find him sitting up
fiddling with the newspaper
scratching tiny hieroglyphics on it.
Mum is sitting on her walker seat
by his bedside, not catching my eye.
'I'm so pleased he is feeling better'
I tell her,
'But you were right to call'.
The next evening, she phones again.
Tells me tearfully
he's the same as he was yesterday.
She thinks she's losing him.
Can I come over?

Dark

On this dim Sunday afternoon
I find my mother dazed in her chair,
ear plugs in, face blank.
My father's door has been shut
the light turned off.
She says all day he's shouted at her.

Bird Food

She says the birds depend on her.
She struggles out over the uneven path
jerking back the rickety door
to find bird food.
With shaking hands
she pours dun sunflower hearts
into the open mouths of the feeders.

He calls out he's lonely.
Some days only the carers
go in to him, to feed, to change him.
He lies face turned away
curled into the side of the cot bumper
refusing to eat until someone
comes and sits with him.

Care System

Under a pile of papers on her table
with small dishes of pills, some broken in half,
I find a list in her tiny handwriting
that wanders up the page:

need gp to call
 double incontinent
   need referral
 bowel and bladder team
urgent referral
  waiting for SALT assessment
   phone nurse (community) to change dressings
needs dentist
contact adult social services – Dawn
    spec savers date (for me)
 dosset box (pharmacy)
chase up hospital
   make him do his physio
get Aymes powder
ask to unscrew lids
 move from bottom shelf
put phone back in cradle
               (will need in morning)

Bells

She wanted to tell them
about the autumn shore
with the white sun over the leaning boats
in the shallow bay,
where oystercatchers poke and prod
and dotterel run along wet sand
tracing fine chains to the sea.
She wanted to tell them
how they cranked up the Austin
and clattered off on their honeymoon,
trailing strings of tin cans and
'Just Married' fixed to the back.
How they trundled out of London
through the sunken lanes of Suffolk
to the guest house
and the motherly proprietress
stout as a bow-legged gull.
She wants to tell them,
when they say it will be easier for her
if he goes into a home,
about that first day they were married
walking on Dunwich shore,
the tide out
the patterns of sandbars
salt wind in her hair.
And how they heard them,
unmistakable, the sound of bells
ringing from the lost church
deep under the sea.

Hope

I get a work email from a mother.

'My daughter was skipping round the room last night.
She thinks we are going to be allowed to stay.'

I know this oblique, Home Office holding response
and how much is invested in the casual words and actions
of others – yesterday the carer
                     left my mother's walker out of her reach.

Lives pass in these files, stacked in the cabinet still open –
clamped down with dog-leg metal levers –
days that stretch ahead flickering like invisible rain falling through leaves

waiting for something,
                a change somewhere in the future.

Snail

Under the porch light on a damp evening
in full view on the front door,
a tiny apricot snail is curled in its shell
oblivious to its precarious position.

So easily knocked, like their frail dog.
Deaf, blind, lying in everyone's path,
sensing only blurred shapes,
she scrabbles up as we step over her.

We debate what to do with her –
where she should go – who will pay for her care –
which of us has the time
to look after an old incontinent creature?

Batteries

The landline phone is ringing
in the front room.
It's in the cupboard with the door closed.
No one phones on it,
except cold callers and Mum.
I hear its faint plaintive muted call
persistent – like the smoke alarm
when it squeals for batteries.
Once we took a bleeping alarm
off the ceiling, but it carried on –
intermittent – a slow piercing note.
I wrapped it in towels
and put it under the stairs
but we could still hear its
muffled calling.
Eventually I took it,
still wrapped up, out to the car
and parked down the road.
Then I forgot about it and when
we came back the next morning,
it was dead.

Resistance

When she stops phoning
and I find her lying back listlessly,
pliantly, in her chair
and she says,

'I need help'
'Can't manage any more'.

My resistance breaks,
like a stook of brittle spaghetti bent into a pan,
a wicker basket handle come undone.

VI.
Grace

In Decline

To start with there was an odd word
left like a fridge on a street corner,
not where you'd expect,
but easy enough to explain.
Then we noticed whole sentences
being wedged into strange places,
a collection of beer cans glittering
in an otherwise ordinary winter privet hedge.
Flocks of scattered thoughts began to
sweep in and out of conversations.
Little fledgling starlings running criss-cross
over a fast-food car park, shallow waves
converging on crumbs, dispersing
dodging feet.
But now and then, in a street
of de-gentrified Victorian villas,
peeping out from among the armchairs
and cars with tyres sunk as pumpkins left out on walls,
there'd be a flash of stained glass
a detail of fine cornice
a still recognisable phrase.

Frame

From his position in bed
he studies the gap
       where the cuff of a jacket
has stopped the wardrobe door from closing.

'Has that car broken down over there?'
                 he asks.

'The garage door doesn't shut.'

I feel his language detach.
The words are displaced,
skewed to one side,
like the window frames
when he mended the sash cords.
I'd watch him lean out backwards
from the upstairs gap
and lift out the window.
It rested, tilted across his legs –
the garden and sky,
my house hanging wonky.

Metaphor

'There's a kite stuck in that tree.'
I look outside the window
at a bright triangle of green light
where the dark trunk of a tree forks,
and I see it too.
Is he using a metaphor? sharing a thought?
I grasp its flimsy beating frame
as the light shifts and the kite is snatched away,
his sentences unreeling fast
zigzagging out over a panoramic scarp.
I am hanging on to him,
to that tiny figure of speech
that might link him back to us
the string stretched as far as it will go.

Forest Canopy

He is retreating to the tops of tall trees
into the forest canopy.
His sentences are expanding
into a labyrinth of hanging ferns
and undiscovered lichens,
of aerial trunks and buttress branches,
fusing together into new walkways
far above the forest floor.
His language has become
its own ecosystem
high up in the roof of the cloud forest
broken free from the ground.

Grace

The Aymes powder spins in the beaker
as I mix and take it through.
We shift him up the bed, prop pillows behind.
I raise the spout to his mouth –
his arm stretches out to steady it,
but then he stops and says the Grace.

His body is pared away, it's thin as a pencil,
shaved down to concave bone.
I lift again the clotted constellation,
a galaxy of yellow specks in a pearl grey sky.

The words have come to him instinctively,
fluently, a pattern ingrained to his core.
The unravelling of a person
a strand of wood, fluted with tips of gold.

Pigeon

I brace myself to go into his room
each time I visit,
the way I brace myself every time
I cross the side road
near the fishmongers.
Once when I was waiting to cross,
an old pigeon had sat on the kerb
and a car cut the corner
rolling over it.
There was the sound
of a crisp bag popping.
The pigeon still there, alive
but flattened like a bath toy
tethered to a red buoy.
Its head and neck still intact.
It wouldn't stop nodding, nodding.
The fishmonger
in his black beanie,
was unloading
white dripping polystyrene boxes
that sprayed arcs of water
in the cold sunlight.

Bycatch

Indistinguishable, like dying fish,
old men lie there, long faces
silver heads and black triangular mouths.
They are the bycatch of a trawler
that has dragged its weighted nets
and steel rollers through their lives,
torn up fragile habitats
and the symbiosis
of ancient partnerships.
I scan each bed on the dementia ward for you
and as my eye adjusts,
I see there, among the indiscriminate waste,
each rare species.
Here a grand aged Leatherback
there, a Roundnose Grenadier
and this one Orange Roughy
that has taken ninety years to mature.

Sketch

I've rescued a drawing
from my studio floor,
a rough sketch of my father
done just a few years ago.
I've captured him
as a kindly jovial friar
who has welcomed old age,
in baggy trousers, belly over
a rough knotted belt,
at peace with his slower life.
Gregorian chant of bees
in the tonsured poppies –
he's stopped to rub his back
leaning on the hoe.
I've drawn his foot
pressed up against the paper's edge
as if to stop the image drifting.

Sponsored Walks

Past the strip of field with the Belted Galloways
between the trainline and the bypass
and the small stone trapezium that marks
where the last highwayman was hung –
the traffic is slowing – and I look for a turn off
find myself on a cut through.

And then I see it, the Women's Refuge
my father fundraised years ago to build.

The refuge is on his list of –
                    'Things I'm most proud of'.

But tied to a post out front there's a commercial sign,

'Acquired by Developers'.

I'm on my way to the hospice to see him
but I pull over and stop.

I think of all the money he raised
all the miles walked.
The final stretch, so tired, the light becoming undone,
trudging back behind panelled garden fences –
back always to the carparks where we began.

Lane

Home from work,
sleeves rolled up in the cool evening,
he'd steady me on my new second-hand bike
along the flat lane
where damp rose from the water-rat stream.
First crossing the busy road,
he'd gather up the bikes by their handle bars
and carry them over,
while we held his other hand and sleeves.
He'd start me off,
hand on the back of the torn plastic saddle
until, imperceptibly,
our whole life together passing,
I found he'd let go.

Installation

I close the door to his room
which had stayed propped open
throughout his illness, and behind it
find a few of his things.
His heavy brown shoes angled
as if he's just taken them off,
jacket and cap hung on the peg,
walking stick against the wall.
Mechanically,
as a bulldozer collapses a site,
we'd removed from the wardrobe
stacks of folded clothes.
But here, behind the bedroom door,
I've stumbled across
this tiny installation of his life –
the space between the objects
protected like a small urban park.

Elegy

He bends into the wind
through shoals of skirting leaves
lifting each knee slowly, using two sticks
to propel himself forward along the track.

But as we arrive at his favourite café in the woods,
to have lunch at the silver-weathered tables
the long queue parts for my father to pass
through to the front. He smiles. Raises his hat.

Everyone knows this kind elderly man –
his hair flying out as wind surges above
in the huge lime and yellow leafed trees.
They've watched over his ageing.

I think of the small ripple that will spread out
with the news that he has died – the weight of daily life
held back momentarily – as someone remembers
something he had done that had helped them.

'You're like Moses, Dad,' I say.
'Look, the Red Sea is parting for you.'

Acknowledgements

Thank you to the editors of the following journals and magazines for first publishing these poems:

'Removal' and interview with Rev. Steve Morris, *Acumen* 95; 'Hope', an early version, *Poetry Birmingham Literary Journal* #1; 'Noah', *Orbis* #199 and *Readers' Choice* #200; 'Evacuees', *The London Magazine* online 2022; 'Bike', *Wildfire Ezine* 2023; 'Forest Canopy' and 'Muster', *Under The Radar* #31; 'Last Vaudeville' (earlier title 'Boat Trip') & 'Taking Leave', *The Spectator* 2023; 'Links', and How I wrote this Poem interview with Zoe Brigley, *Poetry Wales* 2023; 'Visiting' and 'In Decline', *The Spectator* 2024; 'Coda', *Berlin Lit* 2024; 'Printer', 'Ellen Maud Smith' and 'Lane', Featured Poet in *East Ridge Review* and in *Twenty-four Anthology 2024*; 'Handkerchiefs', *Ver Prize Winners Anthology* 2024; 'Batteries', *The Alchemy Spoon* #13; 'Walking Stick', *The Passionfruit Review* 2024; 'Installation', *The Spectator* 2025; 'Pigeon' *The Poetry Review* #115.1; 'Bells', 'Plums' and 'Bycatch', *The Passionfruit Review* 2025; 'Gift' and 'Listening', *Bad Lilies* #20, 'Last Stand', *Magma* #92. 'Ocean World', *ARC Poetry Canada* #107; 'Chrism' *Reach Poetry* #316.

The following poems have won prizes or been placed in these competitions:

'Protest', shortlisted for The Alpine International Poetry Prize 2022; 'Disorientation', longlisted for the *Rialto* Nature & Place Competition 2022; 'Gift', highly commended in the Patricia Eschen Poetry Prize 2022, shortlisted for the Plough Prize 2024 and longlisted for the National Poetry Competition 2024; 'Ellen Maud Smith', shortlisted for the Keats/Shelley Poetry Prize 2023; 'Printer', First Prize in the *East Ridge Review* Winter Green Poetry Competition 2023 and Nominated for the Best of the Net 2024; 'Walking Stick', highly commended in

The Passionfruit Review Poetry Competition 2024; 'Batteries', longlisted for *The London Magazine* Poetry Prize 2024; 'Plums' and 'Bycatch', both were highly commended in *The Passionfruit Review* 2025; 'Sketch', Second Prize in the EHP Barnard Poetry Competition 2025, 'Chrism', Second Prize in the Indigo Dreams Spring Poetry Prize 2025; 'Path', Runner Up in the Wirral Open Festival of Poetry Prize 2025; 'Removal' ('Path, Last Stand and Disorientation') shortlisted for The Alpine International Poetry Prize 2025.

Thanks

I would like to express my heartfelt thanks to the following:

To the Hawthornden Foundation for a 2025 Fellowship which gave me the space and time in Hawthornden Castle to draw the collection together and complete it.

To artist Elizabeth Morris for allowing me to use her etching, 'Fishers of Men' as the cover.

To Jane and Angela and the Nine Arches team for all their support, dedication and expert skills in bringing *Bycatch* to fruition.

To my poetry communities at Ann Pilling's Poetry Group and The Brondesbury Stanza group for the careful readings of many of these poems.

To Rev. Steve Morris and Dr Kawal Singh for reading the manuscript and providing invaluable feedback and advice.

To my friend and mentor Prof. Peggy Ellsberg for her reading and encouragement from the first poems to the last.

I would like to acknowledge the love and care given to my parents by three generations of our extended family, and to the carers and friends who were there for them in their hardest times.

Lastly and most of all I want to thank my husband Barry, for all the hours of love he has spent reading drafts and encouraging me in the writing of this book.